CHRISTMAS
Here, There, and Everywhere

CHRISTMAS
Here, There, and Everywhere

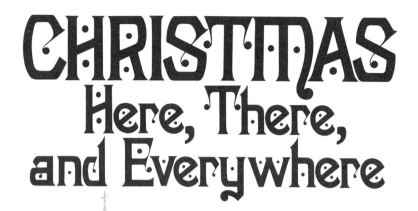

Written and illustrated by
FRANK JUPO

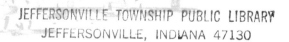

DODD, MEAD & COMPANY
New York

Copyright © 1977 by Frank Jupo

Printed in the United States of America
1 2 3 4 5 6 7 8 9 10

Library of Congress Cataloging in Publication Data
Jupo, Frank.
    Christmas here, there, and everywhere.

    1. Christmas—Juvenile literature.   I.   Title.
GT4985.J86   394.2′68282   77-3893
ISBN 0-396-07462-6

"Happy holidays!" calls Mr. Peters.

"Look at all those presents!" laughs Mrs. Kaye.

"Merry Christmas!" Danny shouts.

"I helped trim the tree!" Kate says proudly.

Everybody is happy. The air is full of joy. It's Christmas, the birthday of Jesus, and for Christians the world over it is a time to celebrate.

The middle of winter has been a time for celebration down the ages—even in the long-ago past when the world was a wilderness and people were pagans. But in those days, people were not celebrating the birth of Jesus. They were celebrating the rebirth of the sun.

Each year, in December, when the nights began growing shorter and the days growing longer, people held a great festival. They put their labors aside and danced and made merry to celebrate the return of the sun.

AN OLD CUSTOM

When holy men set out to preach Christianity to the world, they borrowed that pagan festival to celebrate the birth of Christ. All at once the world had a new holiday.

Along with Christianity, the new holiday spread. And because Christians went to church to attend Mass on that day, the new holiday was soon known as Christmas.

A NEW FAITH

Nowhere was Christmas greeted with greater joy than where winters were hard—where nights were long and days were short and gloomy.

On windswept hills and frozen coasts, people in the north of Europe lit huge fires—as some still do today—and sang and danced to greet the holiday.

TIME OUT TO FROLIC

The celebration never seemed complete without plenty to eat and plenty to drink. Come Christmas—then as now—people put away tremendous meals.

Common folk, hungry most of the year, saved up to stuff themselves just this one time. Nobles and kings feasted on boar's head, partridge, and roasted meats—to the sound of music.

And always there were puddings and pies for everyone. And always there was cake.

TIME OUT TO FEAST

FOR THE NOBLES

FOR THE KINGS

FOR THE PEOPLE

Leftover Christmas cake, nicely powdered and dissolved in water, was the best cure for any ill—or so people believed.

They also believed that boughs of evergreens nailed to the house door kept evil spirits out on Christmas Eve.

When the Church declared this custom unchristian, people were unwilling to go without that holiday greenery. So they moved it indoors.

Ever since, homes have been decorated for Christmas with holly or ivy or mistletoe—anything green that will last.

One Christmas Eve, someone put up a fir tree instead—in a land where firs abounded. And to please his children, he trimmed it nicely with apples and candles.

That was how the Christmas tree came about—some four hundred years ago, in a small German town.

SOME MAKE MERRY

Life in those days was pretty drab, for all but a few. Most people were poor, their days all work and little rest. Only at Christmas did people allow themselves a break.

In some parts of Europe the celebrating went on for weeks. Townfolk and peasants alike dressed up in masks. Some played games or danced in the streets. Others spent the day watching minstrels perform the Christmas story, under the skies, in the marketplace.

SOME ENJOY THE GOINGS-ON IN THE STREETS

In some places countyfolk were treated to a holiday dinner in their lord's manor. But they had to bring their own firewood. Guests found empty-handed got their portions uncooked and unbroiled.

Children everywhere were free to do much as they liked around Christmas time.

SOME DRESS IN COSTUMES

OTHERS PLAY GAMES

German youngsters put on fancy costumes. Schoolboys in England were allowed to lock out their teachers for one day. And in Italy some churches held a Christmas service where boys and girls were permitted to preach.

Then, as now, rich and poor alike knew the joy of giving presents.

Giving gifts—like the Magi on that first Holy Night—was a cherished custom back in Roman times.

So was eating "honeyed things" we call them sweets—on the holidays. Some preferred gingerbread figures, others giant-sized cookies. Some delighted in almond-paste sweets, known as *marzipan*. Others all but stuffed themselves on raisin cake they called *stollen*. To the English, there was nothing like puddings and pies.

All through the holidays, crowds, munching sweets, thronged the streets everywhere, cheering jugglers and puppeteers, and the town's craftsmen marching proudly in parade.

SPECULAAS
Holland

MARZIPAN
Sweden

STOLLEN
Germany

PLUM PUDDING
England

"DECK THE HALLS"

"O COME ALL YE FAITHFUL"

"THE FIRST NOEL"

"JOY TO THE WORLD"

By and by, the celebrating got so out of hand that for a time in seventeenth-century England, celebrating Christmas was forbidden by law.

But if rulers could ruin the joy, they could not silence the singing. When people feel good, they feel like singing. And feeling good at Christmastime, people sang songs, handed down to them by their parents.

Simple tunes for simple folk, most seemed not fit to be sung in church. So groups of singers and musicians began walking the Christmasy streets, sounding off with old shepherd songs, lullabies, and country dances—and pausing in places for a reward.

That was how carols began.

When people left the Old World to settle in America, they brought their Christmas customs along, carols and all.

The Dutch played games like candle-jumping, and also feasted the poor. Scandinavians toasted one another around a blazing Yule log. The Germans lighted their Christmas trees.

THE DUTCH

THE SWEDES

Only the Puritans in New England frowned on the holiday. They kept their workshops open, their churches closed, and harshly punished those who disobeyed.

THE GERMANS

In old-time America, the Dutch had their *Sinterklaas*, the Germans their *Weihnachtsmann*, like their folks back home. No one had ever heard of Santa Claus, as we know him. Until he came along in the American poem, " 'Twas the night before Christmas"—a jolly old man in a reindeer-drawn sleigh.

Yet there was a real Santa Claus—a bishop who became St. Nicholas (which is where the name Santa Claus comes from), who lived in western Asia sixteen centuries ago.

A goodly man, a Saint with a day named after him, he was adored as a giver of gifts and the patron of children and sailors.

"SOME CALL ME SINTERKLAAS!"

"SOME CALL ME SANTA CLAUS!"

As the legend goes, he is still making the rounds at Chris-mas time, leaving gifts under bushes, on window sills, or stuffed into boots or stockings—any place where people might look for them, in keeping with their customs.

IN SPAIN—IT'S SLIPPERS TO HOLD EXPECTED GIFTS

IN FRANCE AND ENGLAND—IT'S BOOTS AND STOCKINGS

For throughout the world, customs are different, and dif-ferent people celebrate Christmas in different ways.

IN RUSSIA—IT'S GRANDFATHER FROST   IN GERMANY—IT'S DER WEIHNACHTSMANN

And various countries know Santa by various names. In England he is Father Christmas, in Russia he is known as Grandfather Frost, and the French call him Père Noël.

In some places he travels in company. In Holland, it's with his servant Black Peter, much beloved by all children. In the Tyrol, it's a devilish creature called Krampus, who haunts the Alps. The Danes love their Santa's helpers, the Nisser, who are his companions, along with his cat.

IN HOLLAND—IT'S SINTERKLAAS AND IT'S BLACK PETER

WHILE KRAMPUS IS MAKING THE ROUNDS IN THE AUSTRIAN ALPS—

Swiss youngsters are treated to a Santa traveling with boy bodyguards balancing strange-looking lanterns on their heads.

But Santa is not always all whiskers and boots. In Italy, on Twelfth Night, the person of Santa Claus comes as a lady— a friendly witch known as Befana. In Portugal, the Magi take Santa's place.

—YOUNG FOLK IN MASKS PARADE IN SWITZERLAND

TOBACCO FOR HIS PIPE

A LUCKY PENNY

GIFTS FOR SANTA

Some grateful folk leave their Santa gifts in return—a lucky penny, tobacco for his pipe, or a plate of pancakes for his helpers, put up on the roof.

Nor do people forget the animals and the birds.

GIFTS FOR HIS HELPERS

A BOWL OF HOT PORRIDGE

A PLATEFUL OF PANCAKES

Belgian children leave a carrot and water for Santa's horse. Polish farmers present their cows with gifts of bread and salt. And dog-lovers in Albania reserve the first piece of Christmas cake for their pets. In Norway birds even have their own Christmas tree, festooned with tasty grains.

Some people have a strange way of giving gifts. The Dutch like to hide them in closets or in the cellar.

SPRUCING UP FOR THE HOLIDAYS

THE FINNS

GIFTS FOR THE BIRDS

Sometimes—if small—they even hide them in cakes. In Norway all you get might be a tiny fun present grandly wrapped up in bundles of paper. Youngsters in Puerto Rico, more lucky, get presents twice—once on Christmas from Santa, once from the Three Kings on Twelfth Night, which is January 6.

THE POLES

Wrapping gifts and getting things ready, young and old everywhere prepare for the holidays. The Dutch scrub their houses. The Finns steam themselves clean in a hot room they call a *sauna*. As a reminder of the Holy stable, Polish peasants scatter straw on the kitchen or bedroom floor.

SOME TOIL WITH SOAP AND BROOM

SOME CHEER THEIR QUEEN

And farmfolk in parts of the Alps take up woodcarving for a while, turning out lifelike Christmas scenes—a skill that has brought them worldwide fame.

Wherever people believe in Christmas, they celebrate.

Some celebrate on St. Nicholas Day on December 6, some on December 25, others on Twelfth Night, twelve days later. But they all like processions and all love parades.

Swiss boys get a great welcome when they come marching, singing old tunes.

SOME TOIL WITH CARVING TOOLS

Swedish towns observe the first day of the Christmas season as St. Lucia's Day, and select a young girl as Lucia. Robed in white, she is paraded through the streets, wearing a crown of lighted candles. And Yugoslavs, like some others, bring home a Yule log from a nearby wood. An old custom, the Yule log is then set alight so that people may wine and dine by the cheerful blaze.

SOME CHEER THEIR YULE LOG

THEY CELEBRATE ON THE MOUNTAINS

In another part of the world, in Africa, Christians greet Christmas with no less joy. In the hills of Ethiopa singing crowds stay up all night to see Christmas dawn. In Nigeria youngsters sing and make music around the clock and perform plays in the streets. And children in Ghana proudly put on their tribal robes for the holidays.

Nearer to our shores, in the Caribbean, islanders decorate their homes with flowers, paper garlands, and colored lights, and celebrate Christmas for weeks.

In Puerto Rico, carolers—known as *trullas*—move from house to house serenading friends and neighbors. Between making music and feasting and going to church, few find the time to sleep.

IN MEXICO—PIÑATA PARTIES

Puerto Rican youngsters are allowed to play practical jokes on grownups and to make, unpunished, as much noise as they please. Real experts use empty tin cans and sticks.

For Mexican children the high point of the season is the breaking of the *piñata*, a fancy-shaped cardboard or pottery jar, filled with small gifts and candies. The trick is—you have to crack it open with a stick, blindfolded, while the jar is pulled up and down.

—AND POSADAS

Piñata parties mark the end of the procession known as *posada*—when parents and children parade through the home or meet friends and neighbors to promenade through the streets, carrying candles and singing hymns, every night for nine nights.

In Guatemala, youngsters in ancient costumes are the pride of the yearly Christmas parade. In Honduras, they say "good-bye" to the holidays with fireworks.

IN PERU—ANCIENT DANCES

IN GUATEMALA—ANCIENT DRESS

SOME PLAY GAMES FOR DAYS AND DAYS

Up in the Far North, in Canada, Eskimo villagers get together to dance for days or play games, while in Newfoundland, each Christmas morning, the men do their good deed by going fishing for the church.

In our part of the world, many observe the holiday the way it is observed in the countries of their forebears.

SOME PARADE TO FIFE AND DRUM

WILLIAMSBURG
Virginia

FOR MORAVIANS—A SPECIAL TREAT

OLD SALEM
North Carolina

ANY PLACE

FOR THE IRISH—LIGHTED WINDOWS

Some parade to fife and drum by candlelight. Others serve coffee and buns at a "love-feast" in church. Some put up a huge fair. Still others place candles in their windows on Christmas Eve, so that travelers—like Mary and Joseph once —may find their way.

FOR THE ITALIANS—A FAIR

NEW YORK

PIZZAS

MERRY CHRISTMAS

GOD JUL

FROEHLICHE WEIHNACHTEN

When, long ago, some few faithful observed their first Christmas, they did hardly foresee that, in time, Christmas would spread throughout the world. And when they sang their first carols and lit their first trees, who would have thought that people would celebrate the birth of Christ in every corner of the earth one day —and in so many ways.

BUON NATALE

FELIZ NAVIDAD